Do you want to be a successful AI ghostwriter?

This book is for you. It's a combination of novel and how-to, telling the story of a secret ghostwriter while also teaching you everything you need to know about becoming a ghostwriter using AI. You won't find information like this anywhere else. It is important to read the stories so you can understand the difference between a human writer and AI.

At its core, a secret ghostwriter is someone whose contributions are unknown to the general public. They work tirelessly behind the scenes, crafting storylines and characters that leave readers captivated and craving more. Whether it's penning bestselling novels or churning out hit songs on demand, these hidden masters of their craft have an impressive ability to conjure up gripping narratives with seemingly little effort.

With this book, you will have all the tools and knowledge you need to become a successful AI ghostwriter – no matter what your experience level is. You can finally achieve the career you always wanted, and be entertained in the process.

Secret AI Ghostwriter

By Amanda Symonds

Contents

Marie - an AI short story about ghostwriting

We start this how-to book with a short story about a ghostwriter called Marie who is young, attractive and having problems getting taken seriously in her career in Seattle. She embarks on a new career as a ghostwriter and suddenly gains respect and $$$ working on Fiverr. It is written by an AI ghostwriter. I hope you enjoy it.

It was a normal day at the office for Marie. She sat at her desk, trying to focus on her work, but she just couldn't seem to get into it. She had been struggling with this problem for a while now, and it was starting to take its toll.

Marie was a secret ghostwriter. She had started working on Fiverr a few months ago and had found financial success there, but doing all of this under the radar was starting to wear on her. She wasn't taken seriously by her colleagues at work, and she felt like she was constantly fighting an uphill battle.

Today was no different. Marie tried hard to focus on her work, but inevitably she found herself browsing the internet instead. She checked her email and saw that she had a new message from Fiverr. It appeared that someone had hired her to write a ghostwritten report for them. This could be the break that she needed to start feeling better about her career again. As she read the message and saw that the client was from outside of her country, she got excited. This would mean a lot of extra work for her and could give her some needed income to help out with bills.

She felt confident that she could write this report, so she quickly replied to the message and accepted the client. She then set about starting on the project. It took her a few days to complete, but she finally finished it and sent it off to the client for their review.

She was nervous as she waited for a response from them, but eventually, they replied, saying that they were very happy with her work and wanted to hire her again in the future. Marie was overjoyed by this news and finally felt like she was making some progress in her career. She knew that if she continued working hard and improving her skills, she would be able to achieve all of her goals in no time.

To get more insight on ghostwriting, Marie decided to do some research online and read about the experiences of other ghostwriters. She found that there were a lot of different opinions out there, but one thing was clear: ghostwriting could be very lucrative if you knew what you were doing.

It was then that Marie realized that she had everything it took to succeed in this field. She would just need to put in the effort and continue improving her skills. With that, she made up her mind to stick with it and get better at ghostwriting every day, knowing that it was going to help her achieve all of her goals in the long run.

As the content is being written, Marie considers how she can make it more engaging for the reader. She wants to provide them with some value and keep their focus on the content that she's writing. This is something that she has always struggled with, but she knows that if she continues working hard at improving her skills, she will be able to succeed in this field.

The content continues to get written, and Marie is feeling very focused on the task at hand. She knows that this is what she wants to do for the rest of her life, so she is putting in all her effort to make it happen. This focus gives her a sense of purpose that she has been missing for a long time, and she can finally see the light at the end of the tunnel.

Once Marie finishes writing her content, she reads it over one more time to make sure that there are no errors in it. She knows that this is an essential step if she wants her clients to be happy with her work, so she takes the necessary time to ensure that everything is in order.

After all of her hard work, Marie sends the content off to her client and waits for their response. She knows that they could be critical of the work that she has done, but she is prepared for any feedback because this is something that all ghostwriters must deal with on a regular basis.

Thankfully, the client loves her content and hires Marie to write more for them in the future. This comes as a relief to Marie because she was worried that they might not be happy with her work. She is pleased with the fact that she has managed to find another ghostwriting gig so quickly and feels excited about continuing to improve her skills as a writer.

After all of this, Marie takes some time to celebrate her success and reflect on everything that has happened since she first started in ghostwriting. She is happy with the progress that she has made so far and knows that it is just the beginning for her. Her hard work and dedication have paid off, and she can't wait to see what else is in store for her in the future.

Tomorrow is Saturday, but she knows there is another writing gig to do for her client and that she must continue to focus on her goals. With this, Marie makes a mental note that she has what it takes to be successful in ghostwriting, and she is determined to keep going no matter what happens from here on out. She knows that the work of being a ghostwriter is not easy, and working on the weekend is not ideal, but the rewards are more than worth it. And she is going to embrace every single moment of it!

As she opens the front door of her apartment, a wave of relief washes over her, followed by an exhausted sigh. The day has been long and tough, but Marie knows that it is all worth it in the end when she can finally get some time to herself.

She enters her apartment and heads straight for the kitchen, where she pours herself a glass of wine and settles down on the couch. It has been a long time since she's had some peace and quiet, and she is looking forward to relaxing with her glass of wine and finally getting some much-needed rest.

She takes a few sips before closing her eyes and letting out a deep breath. She knows that tomorrow will come early, but she is looking forward to tackling it head on. She makes herself dinner and smiles to herself, feeling grateful for all that she has achieved in just one day. She knows that she is going to keep pushing forward and making her dreams a reality, no matter what obstacles come her way. And for now, at least, this is all she needs to focus on.

The next day, Marie gets up bright and early to begin writing. She knows that there is a lot of work to do, but she is determined to put in her all and make it happen. She starts by getting a fresh cup of coffee and sitting down at her desk to get started on the first piece of content for the day.

As she starts writing, she is focused and driven to create something exceptional. She knows her client will expect nothing less than excellent work, and she is determined to deliver on that promise.

After several hours of hard work, Marie finishes the next piece of content. She takes a moment to read it again and make any final edits, then sends it off to her client. She waits anxiously for their response and is relieved when they tell her that the work is excellent. She goes out to enjoy the rest of the day and meet up with friends.

She knows there will always be challenges and setbacks in this line of work, but she is determined to keep going no matter what.

Ok, let's get back to reality and see how it's done!

How to succeed as a ghostwriter

Becoming a successful ghostwriter takes time and effort. You must approach it with the right attitude if you want to achieve your goals in this field, which requires a lot of hard work. Being able to write is one thing but being easy to get along with is another skill that is essential to your success!

As a freelance ghostwriter, it is essential to have the skills and abilities to be easy to work with. This includes being responsive, communicative, and reliable when collaborating with clients and other coworkers. Being easy to work with can help foster strong relationships and build trust between you and your clients. It also ensures that projects are completed on time and to a high standard, which is vital for maintaining a successful freelance writer career.

Whether you're working independently or within a team of writers and marketers, being easy to work with is one of the most important skills you can have! While this may seem like common sense, many professional writers struggle with issues such as poor communication or disorganization that make it difficult for others to work with them. If you are remote, it can be more difficult to communicate easily with your client, but you need to work hard at it! This includes being responsive, punctual, and reliable when interacting. By responding to messages promptly, checking delivery dates and then delivering work on time, you can build trust and foster positive relationships that are essential for a successful ghostwriting career.

Additionally, it is essential to stay organized and focused in your work so that you can meet deadlines and deliver high-quality results consistently. Whether you're managing your own deadlines or working within a team, having good time management skills will help ensure that projects are completed efficiently and on schedule.

However, with the right dedication and focus on your craft, you can become a successful writer in no time. By dedicating yourself to improving your skills as a ghostwriter and staying true to the craft, you will be able to achieve a level of success that is beyond what you might have ever thought possible.

As you continue to hone your skills and put in the hard work that it takes to succeed, you will find that ghostwriting is an incredibly rewarding way to make a living. Sure, there may be some challenges along the way, but they are nothing compared to all of the benefits that this career has to offer.

If you are someone who is passionate about writing and wants to make a living in this field, then becoming a ghostwriter may be the right option for you. Just remember that it requires hard work, dedication, and persistence if you want to achieve your goals in this profession. All of the best writers out there have worked very hard to get where they are today, and you can do the same if you just put in the time and effort it takes.

Advice from serious ghostwriters

1. Start by building your network and establishing yourself as an expert in your niche. This will help you connect with potential clients who need your services and develop a reputation for delivering high-quality work.

2. Stay up to date on trends and industry news, so that you can effectively craft compelling content that speaks to your clients' target audiences. This is especially important if you're working in a fast-paced field like marketing or tech, where trends change quickly and new innovations are constantly being introduced.

3. Develop excellent writing skills and attention to detail. Being able to write well is essential for any successful ghostwriter, as you will be responsible for crafting engaging content that reads well and conveys your client's message effectively.

4. Be willing to invest the time and effort necessary to master your craft. This may mean doing extensive research, working long hours, or investing in additional training or certifications. But

with determination and persistence, you can become a successful ghostwriter who helps clients achieve their business goals through quality writing services.

Skills necessary for success

In case you missed it, in this chapter, we will summarise the skills that you need to be a successful ghostwriter.

The first thing you need to know if you want to be a ghostwriter is that it's not an easy career path. It takes hard work and dedication if you want to be successful, and there are several skills that you'll need to have or develop in order to succeed. These skills include the following:

1. Excellent writing skills: This may seem obvious, but it's essential that you have strong writing skills if you want to be a ghostwriter. After all, your job involves writing! You should be able to come up with engaging and original content on almost any topic, as well as being able to follow the style and voice of the piece that you're working on.

2. Attention to detail: Since you won't always have access to the client or subject of your writing, it's important that you have impeccable attention to detail. This means double-checking every bit of information in your written work before submitting it,

making sure that everything is accurate and consistent.

3. Time management skills: As a ghostwriter, you'll likely be working on several projects at a time, so it's essential that you have strong time management skills. This means knowing how to prioritize your tasks and manage multiple deadlines as efficiently as possible.

4. Good communication skills: As a ghostwriter, you'll need to communicate effectively with your clients and editors. You'll also likely be working remotely in many cases, so good communication will help keep the lines of communication clear between you and other members of your writing team.

5. Grammar checking and editing are essential. Poor work will not be accepted by your client. A good grammar checker is essential! I use Grammarly.

If you want to be a successful ghostwriter, then it's important that you develop or refine these key skills. And once you do, there are plenty of opportunities out there for talented writers like yourself!

Do some research online and see what types of opportunities are available to ghostwriters in your area. Look on LinkedIn jobs and other online marketplaces and check our later chapter on where to advertise your services.

Then, start building up a portfolio of work and start pitching yourself to potential clients.

Essential rules for persuasive copywriting

When it comes to persuasive copywriting, there are certain key rules that you must always keep in mind. Whether you're writing emails, blog posts, sales letters, or any other type of content aimed at convincing your readers to take a specific action, these essential guidelines will help ensure that your copy is effective and engaging.

1. Start with a strong headline that immediately grabs the reader's attention and communicates the main point of your message. Include important points first.

2. Use clear, concise language that is easy to understand and stays on-topic throughout the entire piece. Write for people who are scanning for information and not reading everything through.

3. Incorporate persuasive techniques like logical arguments, emotional appeals, and social proof to convince your readers to take action. Appeal to the buyer's FOMO by creating urgency. Offer

something free to get their details if they don't want to order (yet).

4. Use a conversational tone that sounds natural and relatable rather than overly formal or stuffy.

5. Break up your content with engaging visuals, such as images, videos, and infographics, to keep readers engaged and interested from start to finish.

6. When possible, personalize your message by addressing individual readers directly and referencing their interests or challenges in a specific area.

7. Be sure to make your call to action clear and easy to find. Whether you're asking readers to buy a product, download a free ebook, or sign up for your newsletter, don't make them work too hard to do it!

8. Finally, always remember that the ultimate goal of persuasive copywriting is to get results - whether that means more conversions, higher sales, or simply more engagement from your audience.

If you want to become a successful persuasive copywriter, it's essential to keep these fundamental principles in mind at all times. With the proper techniques and strategy, you can create powerful content that resonates with your readers and motivates them to take action.

Productivity techniques

As a ghostwriter, my most productive days are when I stayed focused on my writing workflow and I have detailed some useful tips for staying productive throughout the day.

My tips:

Setting specific goals for each writing session is a great way to stay productive and on track. Whether you are working on a large project or tackling smaller tasks, it is important to set clear objectives for each writing session, so that you can stay focused and productive throughout the day.

Breaking up large projects into smaller tasks can also help to keep you productive on the days when you feel like you have a lot of work ahead of you. By focusing on one task at a time and setting smaller deadlines for each phase of your project, it is easier to stay motivated and productive through even the most challenging writing tasks.

Try the Pomodoro technique to break up your writing tasks into smaller, more manageable chunks. This technique involves working in 25-minute increments with short breaks in between, allowing you to focus on one task at a time without getting overwhelmed or distracted by other demands on your time.

To further boost your productivity as a writer, try incorporating music or some simple mindfulness techniques into your routine. Whether you choose to meditate, practice deep breathing exercises, or simply listen to soothing music, like LoFi music.

Setting specific times to return phone calls and emails can also help you minimize distractions and stay productive during your writing sessions. By scheduling specific blocks of time throughout the day to respond to emails or calls, you can focus on getting your writing done without being distracted by other work-related tasks.

Turning off notifications on your phone and computer can also be a great way to minimize distractions and stay productive during your writing sessions. Additionally, finding an inspiring workspace where you feel productive and productive can help keep you motivated throughout the day. Whether it is a quiet corner of your home or a nearby cafe, having the right environment for your writing sessions will help you focus on what matters most – your work.

If you are working to a word count, then be sure to complete the first draft and then have a break and read it out loud. Check your grammar and whether it meets the criteria for the assignment and company. Is the intention clear, does it work with other material from the same client? If you have time, and it is a large assignment like a book, seek feedback from a colleague or writing buddy who is familiar with the assignment and company.

At the end of the day, it is essential to take some time for yourself and celebrate your accomplishments as a writer. Whether you reward yourself with a short break or plan a small celebration with friends and family, taking some time to appreciate all that you have accomplished will ultimately help keep you productive and motivated going forward.

Overall, staying productive as a writer takes planning, focus, and discipline. By setting clear goals for each writing session and taking steps to minimize distractions, you can stay productive throughout the day and meet all of your writing deadlines with ease. Good luck!

Essential editing tricks

Are you looking to take your editing skills to the next level? If so, look no further than our guide on editing tricks that everyone should know. Whether you're editing a blog post, an essay, or a novel, these tips will help you perfect your craft and become a true copyeditor.

It is essential to read your draft out loud, as this will help you catch any errors in grammar, spelling, or punctuation. Additionally, make sure to leave yourself plenty of time for editing – don't try to rush through your editing process if you want to produce the best possible results.

A key editing trick is to eliminate unnecessary words and phrases from your writing. This can be done by reading each sentence slowly and asking yourself whether it adds anything meaningful to the piece. If not, cut it out!

Avoid repetition, cliches and overused expressions as well, as these can make your writing feel stale and unoriginal. Instead, try to use more descriptive language that captures the essence of what you're trying to say. These are easy pitfalls that can quickly ruin the quality of your writing and make it seem amateurish and unprofessional.

Paint word pictures by using vivid, descriptive language that captures the reader's attention. This will not only improve the quality of your writing, but it can also help you stand out from other editors in your field.

It is essential to read your draft out loud, as this will help you catch any errors in grammar, spelling, or punctuation. Does it flow or sound like you are stumbling through the sentences?

Make sure to leave yourself plenty of time for editing – don't try to rush through your editing process if you want to produce the best possible results.

Whether you're editing a blog post, an essay, or a novel, these editing tricks are sure to take your editing skills to the next level. With these essential editing tricks at your disposal, you'll keep clients happy and grow your business.

Develop a freelancing mindset

Freelance writers have certain qualities and attributes that make them successful in the online writing world. These include a strong work ethic, an ability to manage their time effectively, and a mindset that is focused on success.

To be successful as a freelance writer online, it is important to have the right kind of work ethic. This means being self-motivated and driven, working hard even when no one else is watching or pushing you to do so. You need to be able to stay focused on your writing goals, even when things get tough or challenging.

Another key factor in succeeding as a freelance writer online is having good time management skills. This means knowing how to balance your writing projects with other commitments in your life, such as a full-time job or family obligations. It also means setting deadlines for yourself and sticking to them, making sure that you always deliver high-quality work on time.

In addition to having the right work ethic and effective time management skills, freelance writers also need to have the right mindset. This means being confident in your abilities, being willing to take risks and try new things, and believing in your own success. When you approach writing with this type of mindset, it becomes much easier to achieve your goals and be successful as a writer online.

Negotiating with clients

As a ghostwriter, one of the most important skills you need to develop is the ability to negotiate with your clients. This involves communicating clearly about your rates, expectations for the project, and any other terms that are relevant to the work you will be doing.

Negotiating deadlines, asking for revisions or feedback in a timely manner, and ensuring that you always deliver high-quality work are all key aspects of negotiating as a ghostwriter.

Some other tips to keep in mind when negotiating with clients include:

1. Setting clear expectations from the outset. This means being upfront about your rates, project timelines, and any other details that will be important to both you and your client.

2. Communicating effectively throughout the process. This can involve sending regular updates on your progress, addressing any concerns or

questions that your client may have, and responding quickly to any requests for changes or revisions.

3. Being willing to compromise when necessary. While it's important to stand firm on certain terms, several key factors go into successful negotiation with clients. These include being prepared, listening carefully to client needs and concerns, maintaining strong communication throughout the process, and being flexible in your approach.

By approaching each negotiation with these key considerations in mind, you can successfully navigate any potential challenges that arise and build lasting relationships with your clients.

If you are new to negotiating as a ghostwriter, it may be helpful to do some research ahead of time on best practices for negotiation. This can include reading articles or books on the topic, participating in online discussions with other writers or business owners about their negotiation experiences, or talking to others who have worked as ghostwriters in the past.

Once you are prepared and ready to negotiate, it is important to listen carefully to your client's needs and concerns. This will allow you to better understand what they are looking for from you, what they expect in terms of communication and collaboration, and any other factors that may impact the project.

Throughout the process, it is also crucial to maintain strong communication with your clients. This includes regular check-ins on progress and updates on any changes or revisions that may be needed along the way. By keeping a close eye on the project and responding promptly to client requests, you can help ensure that everything runs smoothly and on schedule.

In addition to being prepared and staying in close communication with your clients, it is also important to be flexible in your approach to negotiation. This may mean agreeing to specific terms or rates that you initially weren't comfortable with, but keeping an open mind can help you find a good middle ground that works for both you and your client. Obviously working all night to meet a deadline when you have a day job is going to be difficult but at the end of the day it's negotiable if you want and need to do the work.

Ultimately, being a successful ghostwriter requires excellent negotiation skills. Whether you are working on a large or small project, with a new or established client, it is important to approach each negotiation with confidence, flexibility, and a willingness to compromise when necessary. By doing so, you can build strong working relationships and deliver high-quality work that meets the needs of both yourself and your clients.

Battling imposter syndrome

Do you ever feel like a fraud? Like you're not really qualified to be a professional writer? If so, you're not alone. Imposter syndrome is a common problem for many people, especially writers. This condition can cause self-doubt and feelings of inadequacy, which can hold you back from achieving your goals. In this chapter, we will discuss strategies to combat imposter syndrome and achieve success as a writer! To learn more, keep reading.

The first and most important step to combating imposter syndrome as a writer is to acknowledge that it's a real problem. Imposter syndrome can cause feelings of inadequacy and self-doubt, which in turn can lead you to believe that you are not good enough or qualified to do the things you do. But even though these feelings may be common, they are still inaccurate – remember that just because other people experience this condition does not mean it's any less valid!

Another way to combat imposter syndrome is to talk about your experiences with others. Whether this means confiding in friends or family members or connecting with other writers who have dealt with similar issues, talking openly about your feelings can help to alleviate some of the self-doubt and negative thoughts that come with this condition.

In addition to talking about your experiences, you should also focus on building up your confidence through positive affirmations and goal setting. For example, try writing down a list of your personal strengths or things for which you feel proud. Additionally, set specific goals for yourself – both short-term and long-term – and make sure to hold yourself accountable as you work toward reaching those goals.

Building up your portfolio is essential, so you have a range of examples to show your prospective clients. When you look at your work you will also feel more confident.

In addition to these strategies, there are many other ways to combat imposter syndrome as a writer. Whether it's seeking professional support or simply learning how to reframe your mindset, there is always a way out of this condition. So if you're struggling with imposter syndrome, remember: You are not alone, and it is possible to overcome this issue!

Making money ghostwriting

As a ghostwriter, it is easier to make money than as an author. This is because ghostwriters typically have more experience and expertise in writing, making them better suited for both the writing process itself and marketing their work to potential clients. Additionally, ghostwriters are often able to charge higher rates due to the demand for their services, which means that they can earn more money by doing less work.

The average rates in US$ are :

Ghostwriting fiction and non-fiction books: around $400 per book
Ghostwriting Children's Books: around $300-$500
Ghostwriting a screenplay: $5,000
Ghostwriting plays and poetry books typically cost very little ($100-$250)

While it may seem like a daunting task to break into the world of ghostwriting, with the right skills and approach, anyone can do it.

Lucrative ghostwriting niches

Ghostwriting is a highly lucrative niche, with many potential clients and opportunities for success. There are several different niches within the world of ghostwriting, each offering its own unique set of benefits and challenges. Some of the most common include writing for businesses, writing for authors or musicians, and writing for academics or researchers.

Regardless of which niche you choose to pursue, there are a few key skills that will help you succeed in this business. These include strong research skills, impeccable writing ability, and an understanding of your target client's needs and goals. Additionally, it is important to be able to market yourself effectively and build lasting relationships with your clients in order to maintain a steady stream of work over time.

Examples of less competitive and highly paid niches include:

- Ghostwriting for celebrities: Writing memoirs, autobiographies, and other works for well-known individuals is often a very lucrative opportunity. These projects typically command high fees and can lead to long-term relationships with clients who will continue to come back to you for additional writing services.

- Ghostwriting for entrepreneurs: Many successful business owners lack the time or writing skills to create high-quality content for their businesses. Ghostwriting for entrepreneurs can be a great way to help them achieve their goals while earning a steady income.

- Ghostwriting for CEOs or business executives: Writing speeches, articles, or other materials for high-level executives can be a great way to make money as a ghostwriter. These clients are usually willing to pay top dollar for quality work, and you may even have the opportunity to collaborate with them directly on certain projects.

- Ghostwriting for academics or researchers: Ghostwriting academic papers and research reports is another highly lucrative niche in the world of ghostwriting. This type of work typically involves working with experts in a particular field, conducting extensive research, and writing up findings according to strict formatting requirements.

Overall, there are many opportunities within the world of ghostwriting, making it an ideal niche for writers who want to earn a good income while working on projects that they find truly rewarding. Whether you're interested in writing for businesses, authors, or academics, there is a niche that can match your skills and interests.

Famous ghostwriters

One of the most well-known secret ghostwriters is journalist Bob Woodward, who famously wrote several books with former US President Donald Trump. In an interview on "60 Minutes," Woodward revealed that he had worked closely with Trump to produce his bestseller "Fire and Fury: Inside the Trump White House." He also famously co-authored a number of other bestselling political books, including "All the President's Men" and "Fear: Trump in the White House."

Another notable secret ghostwriter is pop music producer Troy Carter, who is known for writing tracks for some of today's biggest artists, including Lady Gaga and John Legend. In a 2018 interview with Forbes Magazine, Carter revealed that he often works behind the scenes crafting songs based on the ideas and preferences of his clients. He also stressed the importance of keeping his name out of the public eye, as he believes that the focus should always be on the artist, not on their collaborators.

Overall, secret ghostwriters are talented writers who work tirelessly to create compelling stories and memorable musical tracks that enthral audiences around the world. Whether they're crafting bestselling novels or producing chart-topping hits, these talented creatives rightfully deserve recognition for their undeniable talent and wizardry behind the scenes.

Ghostwriting software

Ghostwriting software is an essential tool for ghostwriters, as it allows them to easily organize and manage their writing projects. In today's world, it can be difficult to focus on one thing at a time. With so many distractions around us, it's easy to get sidetracked and push off our writing tasks until later. The good news is that there are tools out there that can help you generate ideas and produce the first draft quickly. Some popular options include Scrivener, Ulysses, and yWriter.

Scrivener is one of the most popular ghostwriting software tools available today. With a powerful word processor, outlining capabilities, and integration with cloud-based storage services like Dropbox and Google Drive, it is a complete solution for ghostwriters of all types.

Jasper AI is an artificial intelligence program that can help you with your writing. It includes features like a creative story template, as well as a non-fiction writing recipe and 50+ templates to help you produce compelling writing. If you're struggling with writer's block, Jasper AI may be able to help you get past it. This link https://jasper.ai?fpr=greenbubz includes a free trial with 10,000 words.

Ulysses is another highly praised ghostwriting software option. This app offers a clean and distraction-free interface with lots of helpful editing tools built in. It also integrates well with Evernote, allowing you to quickly capture your ideas anywhere at any time.

WordHippo is a great resource for writers who are looking for more specialized ghostwriting software tools. This website offers a wide selection of free and paid ghostwriting software tools, helping you easily find the perfect tool for your needs. It includes a thesaurus, which can help you find synonyms for words that you're struggling to think of. It also has a word generator, which can create random words that you can use in your writing. If you're having trouble coming up with ideas, WordHippo may be able to help.

Finally, yWriter is a free ghostwriting software program that is specifically designed for novelists. It has powerful tools for outlining and structuring your writing project, as well as a built-in word processor to help you write and edit your work. With all these features, it's no wonder that many ghostwriters recommend yWriter as their top choice for ghostwriting software.

Whether you are a professional ghostwriter or just starting out in the field, there are plenty of excellent options available when it comes to choosing ghostwriting software. Whether you prefer an intuitive yet powerful app like Ulysses or the more robust capabilities of Scrivener, there is something out there to meet your unique needs.

Amelie - a human short story about ghostwriting

Here is the second short story about a ghostwriter called Amelie who is young, attractive and having problems getting taken seriously in her career in Seattle. She embarks on a new career as a ghostwriter and suddenly gains respect and $$$ after working on Fiverr and getting a new lease on life.

She took a deep breath and said to her boss, "Fine, sir. I'll be there,"

Amelie turned away and was about to leave the office when she heard her boss, Sheraz speak once again.

"Oh and Amelie," he said in the tone which he used to assign her some task. "Do wear something… appealing."

"But, Sir," Amelie started to object.

"I don't want to hear it," said Mr. Sheraz, her boss. "You knew while applying for this vacancy that as my personal secretary, it is your job to go to business dinners."

"Yes, sir," she could not say anything. She left the room with tears stinging her eyes. She did not like how her boss made her feel. She was always particularly uncomfortable in his presence. Amelie lived with her very old and sick parents in Seattle. They could not support themselves as her mother was half paralyzed and her father was bedridden as well. Her parents' failing health had left her family in a series of economic problems. They were under a lot of debt and Amelie had no choice but to take up the first job that she could find.

Being from a religious Christian family, it was expected she would dress modestly. She, however knew that it was just on the basis of her looks that she had been given this job. She was an attractive young woman with light brown skin that brought out her features. People could get lost while gazing in her intelligent hazel eyes..

When Amelie came home, she waved to her parents, then went straight to bed. Her parents looked at each other. Both of them knew that something was worrying their daughter for she usually had a long chat with them after work.

"I'll go talk to her," Amelie's mother said, as she took her wheelchair into Amelie's room.

She was about to enter her room when she heard her sobs. It looked as if the young girl was deeply grieved. Her mother started to worry and hurried inside.

"Amelie, sweetheart," she said. "What's the matter?"

Amelie quickly wiped away her tears for she didn't want her mother to see her like this. She had a blood pressure problem and Amelie didn't want her to get sick with worry.

"It- it's nothing," Amelie said, sniffling, trying to regain her composure.

"Sweetie, I'm your mother," she answered. "I think I know when something is wrong with my own daughter. Come one, you can tell me. Did something happen on the way home?"

Her mother feared the worst.

"No, no, no," said Amelie. "It's nothing much actually."

"Amelie!" said her mother, pushing her to tell her more. "Come on…"

"Well," she said, figuring out that there was no way out of this. "If you just had to do something that was against your morals, would you do it?"

Her mother looked alarmed and asked, "What have you done?"

"Nothing," said Amelie. "You know that I'm just a personal secretary who has to go to dinners and look pretty. So my boss just wants me to do my job. I would probably have to wear something I don't want to. Make jokes with men, give them lively company so we can close off the deal in a good environment."

Her mother sighed. She knew this would happen the instance Amelie applied for this job.

"You know that no man can force you to do what you don't want to," said Judith, her mother. "You are the person who gets to decide that. Remember Amelie, we would never force you to adopt something you don't want to. If you want to do all that, we would never stop you. But you must question yourself, is that really who *you* are?"

"I don't want to dress up for strangers, mother," said Amelie, after pondering over her mother's words for a minute. "But what about giving them company? That's not me either, I'm a very private woman."

"Then you remain that way. Do what makes *you* comfortable," said Judith. She got up, and planted a kiss on Amelie's cheek. "I know you've grown to be a wise woman. Let *yourself* decide what's best for you."

Amelie had already made a decision. She got up and went to her wardrobe and pulled out a modest dress. *I wouldn't let anyone objectify me.*

After she had gotten ready, she put on her formal Blazer on top. Gazing in the mirror, she smiled. Yes, *this was* her.

"Mom, I'm leaving!" she informed her, and then left the house.

When she got to the hotel, her boss was already there at a table. She made her way up to him and he looked her up and down with obvious distaste.

"Sorry I'm late," she said, and nodded to the other guests.

"Ah, so you're Miss Amelie," said one of the men, coming towards her in what seemed like a hug. "Nice to meet you."

She moved backwards as he approached and dodged the hug, as she did not feel comfortable with it, instead, she went with a, "Yes, you too."

The man, who was known as Mr. Porter, felt insulted and scowled at Mr. Sheraz. "This is your secretary?" he said. "I would have thought you had better taste. Awfully rude, this one."

Amelie, who had taken a seat at the end of the table looked up and said, "I'm really sorry if my actions offended you Mr. Porter, but I am from a respectful family and I think you should respect my boundaries."

Mr. Porter was taken aback by the crude reply, but his business partner looked amused. The straightforwardness of this young woman struck his fancy.

"Shall we begin?" said Amelie, getting straight to business. Mr. Sheraz was obviously very displeased with her. Amelie went home. She was sure that had she succumbed to his wishes, she would not be at peace with herself right now.

****

Amelie went to office the next day and approached her boss. As she expected, he had already posted an ad about a vacancy at his firm.

"You, Amelie," said Mr. Sheraz, struggling for words. "You're just too much. You're fired!"

Boom. The bomb had dropped. Her mind wandered off to her father's medical bills which she had to pay. Tears stung her eyes, for being an only child, it was on her to help out her parents. She had done

the right thing so why was God punishing her
instead of rewarding her.

"Please, sir," she said, a pleading note creeping into
her voice. "There must be some way we can come
to a reconciliation?"

"That's my last word," he said, firmly. "You will not
be working here. Go pack up your stuff!"

Amelie was struck with the horrific realization that
she had no source to generate any money from.
Days were spent applying for jobs, taking up
interviews but never receiving a call back. She
began to explore her options. This is where she
decided to start working as a freelancer. She
started up very small and set up her account on
Fiverr, a platform where you can be a ghost writer.

She started working and slowly began to make
decent sum of money monthly, enough for her
parents to get the medication they needed. She
found a permanent buyer, Adam, and began
working with him quite a lot. They talked a lot and
became good friends. He lived in Seattle as well,
and they decided to meet in person.

"Hello, Miss Amelie," he said as he approached her in the cafe.

"Hey", she answered with a shy smile.

They began to talk and then Adam said, "You were doing a job that you didn't want to do, right? Well, I may have just the proposal for you,"

"Proposal?" Amelie asked.

He replied, "As much as I have known you, you underestimate yourself. You have so much to offer …" he paused, then said, "My brother works for a local newspaper company. I believe that someone like you can work her way to the top. Would you be my ghostwriter?"

"You mean…" Amelie asked, surprised. "write for you?"

"I know talent when I see it, trust me," said Adam. "Besides…I can already see the headline of your column on our soon-to-be 'Infamous' Mr. Sheraz,"

This actually brought a smile to Amelie's lips. She could get back at him!

"I'm in," she said decidedly. "When and where do I appear for an interview?"

Adam handed her a business card. "Tomorrow at noon."

After he had left, Amelie stared at the card for about five minutes. Then, she looked up at the sky and mouthed a 'Thank you'. For a moment there, back at the office, she had actually started doubting the justice of God. She had chosen her morals, and now God had opened another door for her.

A few months had passed since Amelie had accepted Adam's call for the job interview. She had found Adam to be extremely friendly and he had made the work environment quite comfortable for her. Every day she would walk into her lavished office with her head held high, all composed and confident. Her life had taken an unexpected turn that she was not expecting. She wrote loads of articles in which she fought for the rights of the women denied to them. Every week a new article of hers would get published, and the public showed a positive response to it. She soon became a renowned columnist and received excellent pay which was more than enough for her father to get his treatment. She was the face of the 'New Woman' that would not sit back and be suppressed by men. Every day, she would lend an ear to new cases of different women, she would listen to their stories and would write articles about them and give a voice to their suppressed words and would bring their suppressers to justice.

It was another such day when she was in her office, and Adam walked in excited, "You won't believe what we have got on our hands!" he said looking at her with a huge smile and twinkling eyes.

"What is it? Spit it out!" responded Amelie. "You know how you have always wanted to get back on Mr. Sheraz? Well, now's your chance, that fool hasn't changed a bit!" said Adam with a clenched jaw.
"What are you talking about Adam, Get back on Sheraz? How?" asked Amelie confused. Adam asked her to hold up for a minute or two and went out of the office, almost running with excitement. Amelie waited and watched the door until Adam walked back in and brought a girl, almost Amelie's age. "This is Eve" he said. He told Eve to tell Amelie what she had told him. Eve began her story of how

she had taken up the job as Mr. Sheraz's secretary and how he had exploited her and how she wasn't able to tell anyone before because she needed the money desperately to support her entire family of seven. Long suppressed anger boiled up in Amelie, she was set on exposing him now. Days and nights she had spent gathering the information and data of all the previous secretaries and writing an article with all the evidence in it. It came as a shock to everyone for Sheraz always portrayed himself to be a decent man. No one had expected such cheap acts from him. Instant action was taken against him, and he had to suffer a lot, he had to go to court and his company and his reputation faced massive loss.

Amelie felt the weight of hatred lift off her chest now, she breathed a sigh of relief and thanked God for all the blessings he had bestowed upon her. She broke this good news upon her mother as well, who, upon hearing it, told her that she knew that it'd happen one day, for injustice never escapes punishment.

Should you use AI software for ghostwriting?

There is no clear consensus on whether or not artificial intelligence (AI) software can be used effectively for ghostwriting. Some argue that AI has the potential to produce high-quality content that rivals that of human writers, while others contend that there are still significant limitations and challenges to overcome when it comes to automated writing.

At this point, the use of AI for ghostwriting largely depends on the specific project at hand. If you are looking to create a long-form piece such as a book or research paper, then you may want to consider working with a professional writer who has experience using various types of AI tools and platforms. However, if you simply need some help creating shorter pieces such as blog posts or social media updates, then there are a number of templates and recipes available that can help you get the job done.

Ultimately, the decision to use AI for ghostwriting will depend on your individual needs and preferences, as well as the specific project at hand. Whether you decide to go with human writers or automated software, it is important to carefully consider all the factors involved in order to achieve the best possible results.

There is no clear answer to whether or not AI software should be used for ghostwriting, as this depends heavily on the individual project and desired outcome. Some might argue that AI has the potential to produce high-quality content that rivals that of human writers, while others might point to the many limitations and challenges associated with automated writing.

At this point, it is important to carefully consider all aspects of your project when deciding whether or not to use AI software for ghostwriting. Factors to consider might include the scope and complexity of your content, your budget and timeline, and your target audience.

Ultimately, the decision will depend on a number of individual factors, including your own preferences and experience with using AI tools. With proper research and careful planning, you can use AI software effectively to create content that meets all your needs and exceeds your expectations.

Can I write using ChatGPT?

Are you looking to take your writing skills and talents to the next level? Well, look no further: ChatGPT offers a unique opportunity to explore the exciting world of ghostwriting. So, if you're curious about how ChatGPT works as a ghostwriter's tool – as well as its advantages and disadvantages – stay tuned! We'll discuss all these topics (and more) in-depth within this chapter!

Ghostwriters can work with Chatgpt, an AI-powered language model that helps them produce high-quality content. Chatgpt provides ghostwriters with a customizable, intuitive, and easy-to-use platform that helps them write compelling content. The process is simple: the client provides the ghostwriter with the necessary information, and the ghostwriter uses ChatGPT to produce a draft, which is then edited and refined until it meets the client's needs.

The benefits of using ChatGPT to write as a ghostwriter are many. With its AI algorithm, you can quickly generate content that is both engaging and well-written. Plus, ChatGPT allows you to tailor your writing to specific industries and niches, giving you the flexibility to take on a variety of projects. And perhaps the best part? You can save time and energy by cutting down on research and editing time. So if you're looking to streamline your ghostwriting process and produce great content at a faster rate, it's great to try the free software.

When it comes to writing assignments, ChatGPT can be a valuable tool to have in your arsenal. However, it's important to know how to use it effectively. One tip is to be specific in your prompts. The more detail you can provide, the better the response from ChatGPT will be. Additionally, take the time to review and edit your responses.

While ChatGPT is impressive in its ability to generate content, it's not perfect. It's up to you to make sure the final product is high-quality and accurately reflects your ideas. Finally, don't be afraid to experiment and try new things. ChatGPT is a versatile tool with a lot of potential, so don't be afraid to get creative and see what it can do!
With the help of ChatGPT, you can write compelling product descriptions, blog posts, social media captions, and more. Not only does this tool simplify

the writing process, but it also produces high-quality content that resonates with your target audience. ChatGPT's advanced technology analyzes your input and generates content that mimics human-like writing, making it difficult for your clients to distinguish between computer-generated and human-written content.

One of the major drawbacks to using ChatGPT is that it lacks the human touch, so you will still need to review and edit your content before submitting it. There are some performance issues using the program and the free version goes offline frequently. So you need to be patient. You will also need to put your content through plagiarism checks and an AI content checker - you will see that your content is detected as AI. Some business clients will not like this at all! You need to upgrade to using a professional AI software like Jasper AI, which cannot be detected as AI content.

Additionally, ChatGPT only supports English language input, so if you're working on a project in another language, you'll have to look elsewhere. And finally, while ChatGPT produces great content quickly, it can sometimes miss important nuances or misinterpret context – so make sure you take the time to thoroughly review each piece of content before submission.

Being a ghostwriter can be a great experience, especially when utilizing AI. Not only does it provide you with the chance to hone your skills as a professional writer but also gives you the opportunity to create engaging content for your clients. Moreover, it can open up doors into new avenues of writing and offer extra income if you play your cards right. Additionally, using tips from experienced ghostwriters is a great way to ensure that you use the service efficiently and produce high-quality work. All in all, using ChatGPT adds excitement and diversity to the writing field and provides opportunities even to those who haven't written professionally before. In short, don't be afraid to take that leap into ghostwriting – with ChatGPT you'll be sure to find success!

Jasper AI

Looking for a secret ghostwriter to help you tell your story? Look no further than JasperAI, the innovative platform that uses cutting-edge artificial intelligence technology to create compelling and engaging content without the need for an actual human writer. It includes features like a creative story template, which I used, as well as a non-fiction writing recipe and 50+ templates to help you produce compelling writing. If you're struggling with writing copy for a client, Jasper AI may be able to help you create compelling copy. This link https://jasper.ai?fpr=greenbubz includes a free trial with 10,000 words.

With Jasper AI, you can trust that your book will be crafted with skill and precision. Using advanced algorithms and machine learning techniques, their platform analyzes your writing style, audience preferences, and other key factors to produce content that truly speaks to your readers. Whether you're looking to pen a novel, non-fiction book or craft the perfect memoir, Jasper AI has got templates and recipes to help you.

Their intuitive platform makes it easy for anyone to get started, and their team of expert writers is always available to answer any questions you may have. The cost is $40 per month, but you can get started for free with their trial. So what are you waiting for? Give Jasper AI a try and see how your story comes to life!

Ethics using AI

When it comes to using artificial intelligence software as a ghostwriter, there are many ethical considerations to take into account. Some clients may be wary of working with an AI program, feeling that their content is somehow less authentic or original when written by a machine instead of a human writer. However, others may not mind at all, and may even prefer the fast turnaround time and consistent quality that an AI software program can offer.

Whether it is ethical or not to use an AI program as a ghostwriter depends on your client's preferences and expectations. If they value authenticity above all else, you may need to disclose using an automated writing tool to maintain trust with your client.

On the other hand, if your client is primarily concerned with getting their content written quickly and efficiently, then using an AI program may be the ideal solution. Ultimately, it is up to you as a writer to determine which approach will work best for your unique clientele and situation.

Short story comparison

Now you have read the two stories about Amelie, you will see distinct differences in the styles of writing. The first story is motivational and doesn't focus on dialogue, as I wrote this story first using Jasper AI to focus more on the main character and her thoughts.

Yes, Jasper AI wrote the Amelie short story at the front of the book himself! He was provided with a short description and some information about the character and her struggle and was able to come up with a story.

The second story was written by a ghostwriter I hired on Fiverr who wanted to introduce the character through dialogue and tell the story from a moral perspective.

You decide what you think about the two stories. What effect do they have on you?

We discuss the challenges to writing with AI in the next chapter.

Challenges to writing fiction using AI

When it comes to writing fiction, there are many difficult aspects that can be challenging for an artificial intelligence like Jasper AI. Some of the biggest challenges include depicting characters and emotions realistically, creating complex plot lines and storylines, and developing a unique writing style that engages readers. However, with advances in machine learning algorithms and natural language processing techniques, it is becoming increasingly possible for AI systems like Jasper to overcome these challenges and produce high-quality fiction content.

One of the biggest hurdles when it comes to writing convincing fictional characters is accurately capturing their emotions and motivations. This requires not only understanding human psychology and behavior but also having sufficient knowledge about the world in which the story takes place. To address this challenge, some AI systems have been trained using large corpora of text that include descriptions of emotions and actions, allowing them to learn the linguistic cues associated with these concepts. Additionally, many modern machine learning algorithms are able to analyze large volumes of text data and generate predictive models based on this information. This allows AI systems to conduct sentiment analysis on fictional characters, measuring their levels of happiness, sadness, anger, and other emotional states in order to better understand what drives their actions.

Creating complex and engaging plotlines is another major challenge for AI systems when writing fiction. This requires having a good understanding of narrative structure, including elements such as conflict, rising action, climax, and resolution. Fortunately, there has been significant progress in natural language generation techniques over the past few years that have enabled machines to produce coherent and cohesive narratives without relying on pre-written templates. For example, some AI systems have been trained using machine learning algorithms that analyze large volumes of text data to identify the important elements of successful storytelling, such as character development, plot pacing, and emotional engagement. With this knowledge, they can then generate new content by combining these characteristics in innovative ways to create truly compelling stories.

In addition to depicting characters and storylines realistically, another key aspect of effective fiction writing is developing a distinct writing style that is both engaging and authentic. This often requires thinking outside the box and experimenting with different narrative techniques in order to capture readers' attention. One approach that some AI systems have used is leveraging neural networks to generate abstract or conceptual images that can be used as inspiration for new storylines or plot developments.

Additionally, many AI systems are also able to analyze large volumes of text data in order to identify popular and successful writing patterns that they can then incorporate into their own work. Overall, the key to overcoming these difficult aspects of fiction writing is utilizing the latest advances in machine learning algorithms and natural language processing techniques in order to create more realistic, compelling, and engaging content.

So, watch this space!

SEO copywriting

SEO copywriting is a key component of any effective SEO strategy. This involves incorporating keywords into your content in a strategic and natural-sounding way that helps to improve your site's search rankings. Clients often want SEO content and are willing to pay more, so the article ranks in Google.
First, we will talk about methods and secondly, about software.

There are many different techniques and best practices for writing effective SEO copy, such as:

1. Including relevant keywords in the title, headlines, subheadings, and body of your content. This will help ensure that search engines prioritize your content when users are searching for those keywords.

2. Using other on-page optimization strategies like internal linking and optimizing images for search engines. These tactics can also help improve your site's ranking in search results pages.

3. Incorporating an element of storytelling into your SEO copy. This can help your content to be more engaging and appealing to readers, which may encourage them to share it online and link back to your site.

4. Creating unique, high-quality content that is tailored specifically for your target audience. This will not only help you improve your SEO rankings but also build trust and credibility with potential customers or clients. Ok, it is not always possible to be unique but it is something to consider.

Of course, you can use AI software to help you with the above best practises.
Use a tool like SurferSEO as you write your content to ensure that you are optimizing it for search engines and making the most of every opportunity to improve your site's rankings. You will see suggested keywords and a score for each article you write. With these tips and best practices, you can create high-quality SEO copy that will help drive more traffic to your client's site and ultimately boost your bottom line. With careful planning and consistent execution, you can create SEO-optimized copy that will help your writing service

stand out from the competition and attract more customers for your clients.

As you can see, there are many different strategies for writing compelling SEO copy. Whether you're just starting out or looking for ways to improve your existing content, there are plenty of tips and techniques that can help you succeed in this crucial aspect of digital marketing.

Places to advertise your writing services

1. Online job boards and marketplaces. Sites like Upwork, Freelancer, and Fiverr are excellent platforms for advertising ghostwriting services online. These sites make it easy to connect with potential clients and showcase your writing expertise.

2. Social media platforms. Using social media is a great way to reach potential clients who may not otherwise be aware of ghostwriting services. Consider posting regularly on Facebook, Twitter, Instagram, or other social channels to promote your ghostwriting services and build your online presence.

3. Email marketing campaigns. Another effective way to promote ghostwriting services is through email marketing campaigns targeted to specific audiences. This can include things like email newsletters, promotional emails, or drip campaigns that deliver helpful content and encourage potential clients to engage with your ghostwriting services.

4. Industry-specific websites and publications. If you specialize in ghostwriting for a particular industry or niche, consider reaching out to relevant websites and publications that offer advertising opportunities. This can be a great way to target potential clients who are already interested in ghostwriting services and may be more likely to hire you as their writer.

5. Online directories and listings. There are many online directories and listings where ghostwriters can advertise their services, including sites like Writerslabs, which offer ghostwriting jobs as well as ghostwriter profiles with contact information. These sites make it easy to connect with potential clients looking for ghostwriting help, so they're a great place to start when advertising ghostwriting services online.

6. Paid advertising. If you have the budget for it, paid advertising can be a powerful way to reach potential clients who are actively seeking ghostwriting services online. Consider investing in ads on Google AdWords or Facebook Ads, or partnering with an influencer whose audience would be a good fit for your ghostwriting services.

7. Offline networking events and conferences. Attending local networking events and conferences related to ghostwriting or writing in general is another great way to connect with potential clients who might need ghostwriting help. Whether you're looking for new ghostwriting clients or simply want to build your network of writer contacts, these types of offline events can be extremely valuable for promoting your ghostwriting services.

8. Industry-specific conferences and events. If you specialize in ghostwriting for a particular industry or niche, consider attending relevant conferences and events to network with potential clients and learn more about the latest trends in your field. This can be a great way to stay up-to-date on the latest ghostwriting needs, as well as connect with other ghostwriters who might have valuable tips and insights to share.

9. Local meetups, workshops, and classes. There are many online and offline opportunities for ghostwriters to connect with others in their field or interested in ghostwriting services - whether through local meetups, writing workshops or classes, or even online groups like Facebook groups dedicated to ghostwriting topics.

These types of events can be a great source of ghostwriting clients, as well as a way to build your network and learn new tips and strategies for ghostwriting success.

10. Collaboration with other ghostwriters. Another smart strategy when promoting ghostwriting services is to partner with other ghostwriters to share resources and reach new audiences. This might include things like co-marketing campaigns on social media, guest posting on each other's websites, or partnering on webinars or educational content that focuses on ghostwriting topics. By teaming up with others in your field, you can broaden your reach and increase the visibility of both your own ghostwriting services and those of your fellow ghostwriters.

Alternative names for a ghostwriter

One alternative name for a ghostwriter is a scribe or an amanuensis.

A scribe is typically someone who is trained to write manuscripts, often for historical or religious purposes. An amanuensis, on the other hand, is a writer who is hired to compose text on behalf of another person. Both scribes and amanuenses are types of ghostwriters, as they are typically paid to provide writing services in situations where their actual authors do not have the time or expertise to produce content themselves.

Other alternative names for a ghostwriter may include words like "ghost author" or "penman." While these terms typically refer to people who write fiction or non-fiction works under their own name, they may also be used to describe other types of writers who create content for others.

Copywriter, ghostwriter, and collaborator are other alternative names that are sometimes used. These terms refer to writers who create content for a specific purpose or audience, such as marketing or promotion.

Copyeditor, editor, and proofreader are also alternative names for a ghostwriter. These terms refer to individuals who review written content for errors or inconsistencies, ensuring quality and accuracy before publication.

Other alternative names for ghostwriters include freelance writer, contract writer, or author-for-hire. These terms all refer to writers who work on a project-by-project basis and are usually contracted by an individual or organization rather than directly employed by that entity.

Whether you're looking to become a ghostwriter, it's essential to understand the different alternative names that are used in this field. Whether you are looking to help write blog posts, marketing materials, or a full-length book, with the proper knowledge and skills, you can succeed as a professional writer in any of these roles.

Getting references

When you are performing a ghostwriting job, you may not be able to get references from the employer. However, there are a few strategies that you can use to get references as a ghostwriter.

One approach is to ask your clients for testimonials or referrals from others they have worked with in the past. You can also for these using your LinkedIn profile and approve them to be visible online. These endorsements can be used to highlight your ghostwriting skills and build trust with potential new clients.

You can provide links to blog articles, brochure copy and online website sales copy that you have written in the past. This will help demonstrate your ghostwriting abilities and give potential employers an idea of the quality work you can produce. The client needs to trust you wrote it.

Another strategy is to build your own portfolio of ghostwriting work. This can include short ghostwriting projects or samples of longer ghostwritten content, such as white papers or case studies. This will help you establish yourself as a reputable ghostwriter and potentially attract new clients looking for ghostwriters with proven experience.

To succeed as a ghostwriter, it is essential to be authentic, reliable, and professional at all times. By focusing on building solid relationships with your clients and providing high-quality ghostwritten content, you can set yourself up for success as a successful ghostwriter.

Another strategy is to develop relationships with other ghostwriters in your field. This could include writers' associations, freelance communities, or other professional networks that you belong to. Networking with others in your industry can help you build connections, share resources and learn new tips and techniques for success. Often, these writers will send jobs your way (referrals) when they don't want to or can't accept the work themselves, allowing you to grow your ghostwriting business and increase your earning potential. A referral from another professional may also mean that your work is recommended/trusted, and often, that small job can go on to become an ongoing client!

Winning some awards or competitions for ghostwriting can also help you establish yourself as a credible ghostwriter and set yourself apart from others. Whether it's through writing organizations or online communities, there are many opportunities to showcase your ghostwriting skills and demonstrate your expertise to potential clients. With persistence and dedication, you can build a successful ghostwriting business that allows you to work on projects that genuinely interest you and make a positive impact in the world.

Ultimately, if you are committed and passionate about ghostwriting, you can build a strong professional reputation and establish yourself as a reliable ghostwriter who consistently delivers high-quality work. By focusing on your skills, building relationships with other professionals, and staying persistent in your efforts, you can find success as a ghostwriter and grow your business over time.

Places to advertise ghostwriting services

1. Online job boards and marketplaces. Sites like Upwork, Freelancer, and Fiverr are excellent platforms for advertising ghostwriting services online. These sites make it easy to connect with potential clients and showcase your writing expertise:

Craigslist

One of the best places to advertise as a ghostwriter online is Craigslist. Craigslist is a website that allows people to post classified ads for free. You can post an ad in the "writing" section and include your contact information and rates.

Fiverr

Fiverr is a website where you can offer your services for any rate you decide. You can create a gig offering your ghostwriting services and include information about your experience and rates. You can create a gig for 1000 words at one price and set a delivery time. You can create a higher priced gig for a book with a different timeframe.

Upwork

Upwork is a freelancing platform that connects businesses with freelancers. You can create a profile and include information about your ghostwriting services, rates, and samples of your work.

PeoplePerHour

PeoplePerHour is another freelancing platform that connects businesses with freelancers. You can create a profile, include information about your services, and set your own rates.

Freelancer

Freelancer is yet another freelancing platform that connects businesses with freelancers. You can create a profile, include information about your services, and set your own rates.

Guru

Guru is another freelancing platform that connects businesses with freelancers. You can create a profile, include information about your services, and set your own rates.

Hubstaff Talent

Hubstaff Talent is a website that connects businesses with remote workers. You can create a profile and include information about your ghostwriting services, rates, and samples of your work.

Toptal

Toptal is a website that connects businesses with the top 3% of freelance talent. You can create a profile and include information about your ghostwriting services, rates, and samples of your work.

No matter which platform you choose, it's important to be professional and responsive when communicating with potential clients. Ultimately, the key is to build strong relationships with your clients and provide high-quality ghostwriting services that are valued by the market. Good luck!

2. Social media platforms. Using social media is a great way to reach potential clients who may not otherwise be aware of ghostwriting services. Consider posting regularly on Facebook, Twitter, Instagram, or other social channels to promote your ghostwriting services and build your online presence.

3. Email marketing campaigns. Another effective way to promote ghostwriting services is through email marketing campaigns targeted to specific audiences. This can include things like email newsletters, promotional emails, or drip campaigns that deliver helpful content and encourage potential clients to engage with your ghostwriting services.

4. Industry-specific websites and publications. If you specialize in ghostwriting for a particular industry or niche, consider reaching out to relevant websites and publications that offer advertising opportunities. This can be a great way to target potential clients who are already interested in ghostwriting services and may be more likely to hire you as their writer.

5. Online directories and listings. There are many online directories and listings where ghostwriters can advertise their services, including sites like Writerslabs, which offers ghostwriting jobs as well as ghostwriter profiles with contact information.

These sites make it easy to connect with potential clients looking for ghostwriting help, so they're a great place to start when advertising ghostwriting services online.

6. Paid advertising. If you have the budget for it, paid advertising can be a powerful way to reach potential clients who are actively seeking ghostwriting services online. Consider investing in ads on Google AdWords or Facebook Ads, or partnering with an influencer whose audience would be a good fit for your ghostwriting services.

7. Offline networking events and conferences. Attending local networking events and conferences related to ghostwriting or writing in general is another great way to connect with potential clients who might need ghostwriting help. Whether you're looking for new ghostwriting clients or simply want to build your network of writer contacts, these types

of offline events can be extremely valuable for promoting your ghostwriting services.

8. Industry-specific conferences and events. If you specialize in ghostwriting for a particular industry or niche, consider attending relevant conferences and events to network with potential clients and learn more about the latest trends in your field. This can be a great way to stay up-to-date on the latest ghostwriting needs, as well as connect with other ghostwriters who might have valuable tips and insights to share.

9. Local meetups, workshops, and classes. There are many online and offline opportunities for ghostwriters to connect with others in their field or interested in ghostwriting services - whether through local meetups, writing workshops or classes, or even online groups like Facebook groups dedicated to writing topics. These types of events can be a great source of clients, as well as a way to build your network and learn new tips and strategies for success.

10. Collaboration with other ghostwriters. Another smart strategy when promoting writing services is to

partner with other writers to share resources and reach new audiences. This might include things like co-marketing campaigns on social media, guest posting on each other's websites, or partnering on webinars or educational content that focuses on ghostwriting topics. By teaming up with others in your field, you can broaden your reach and increase the visibility of your own ghostwriting services and those of your fellow ghostwriters.

Conclusion

I have you have been motivated to push ahead with your desire to become a ghostwriter. It is a rewarding job, and if you don't mind being anonymous, then it could be the ticket for you. Good luck with your career!

Please remember to leave a review so others can find this book!

www.ingramcontent.com/pod-product-compliance
Lightning Source LLC
Chambersburg PA
CBHW072153020426
42334CB00018B/1990